To parents and teachers

We hope you and the children will enjoy reading this story in either English or French. The story is simple, but not simplified so the language of the French and the English is quite natural but there is lots of repetition.

At the back of the book is a small picture dictionary with the key words and how to pronounce them. There is also a simple pronunciation guide to the whole story on the last page.

Here are a few suggestions on using the book:

- Read the story aloud in English first, to get to know it. Treat it like any other picture book: look at the pictures, talk about the story and the characters and so on.

- Then look at the picture dictionary and say the French names for the key words. Ask the children to repeat them. Concentrate on speaking the words out loud, rather than reading them.

- Go back and read the story again, this time in English and French. Don't worry if your pronunciation isn't quite correct. Just have fun trying it out. Check the guide at the back of the book, if necessary, but you'll soon pick up how to say the French words.

- When you think you and the children are ready, you can try reading the story in French only. Ask the children to say it with you. Only ask them to read it if they are keen to try. The spelling could be confusing and put them off.

- Above all encourage the children to have a go and give lots of praise. Little children are usually quite unselfconscious and this is excellent for building up confidence in a foreign language.

Published by b small publishing
This new edition published in 2018
www.bsmall.co.uk
© b small publishing, 1996, 2018
1 2 3 4 5
Design: Lone Morton and Louise Millar
Editorial: Catherine Bruzzone and Susan Martineau
Production: Madeleine Ehm
Printed in China by WKT Co. Ltd.
ISBN-13: 978-1-911509-54-7
British Library Cataloguing in Publication Data. A catalogue record for this book is available from the British Library.

Happy birthday!

Bon anniversaire!

Mary Risk
Pictures by Lucy Keijser
French story by Jacqueline Jansen

b small publishing

It's my birthday.

C'est mon anniversaire.

Here are all my friends.
Hi! Hello! Come in, everyone!

Voilà tous mes amis.
Salut! Bonjour! Entrez tous!

All these presents for me?
What a brilliant mask!

Tous ces cadeaux pour moi?
Quel masque génial!

And I love this dinosaur!

Et j'adore ce dinosaure!

Let's blow some bubbles.
Aren't they lovely?

Si on faisait des bulles de savon?
Elles sont belles, non?

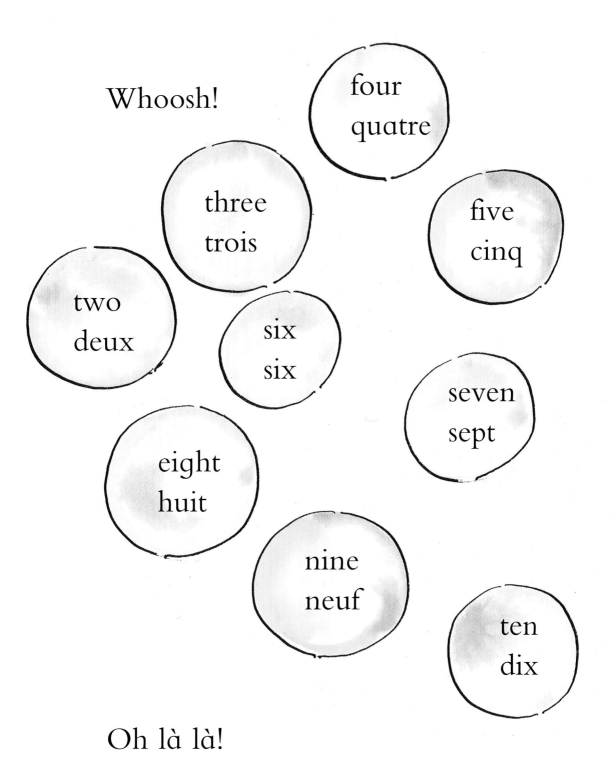

Where have they all gone?

Où sont-elles passées?

Oh! look at Sarah!

Eh! Regardez Sarah!

Balloons!
Can I have one?

Des ballons!
Est ce que je peux en avoir un?

The red one's for you.
Le rouge est pour toi.

The green one's for me.
Le vert est pour moi.

The blue one's for Peter.
Le bleu est pour Pierre.

The purple one's for Clare.
Le violet est pour Claire.

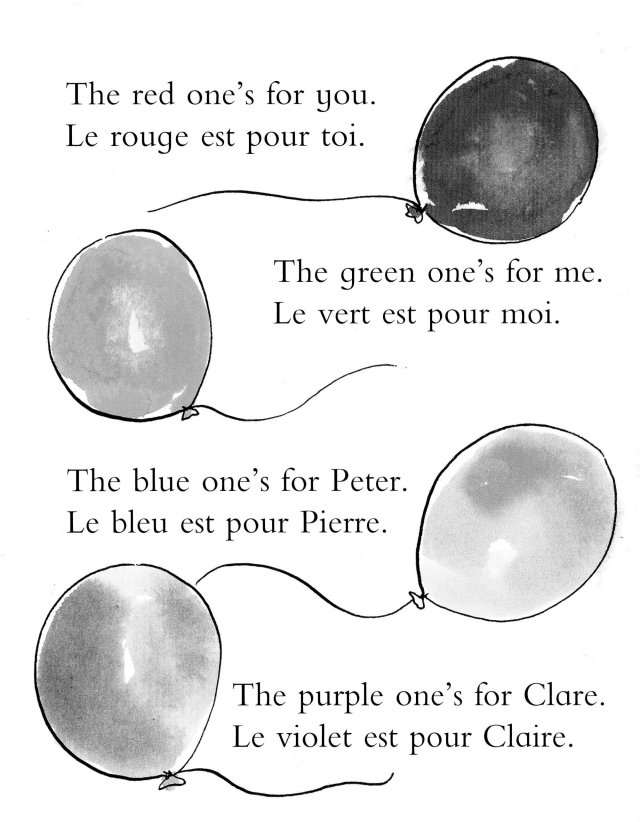

This is fantastic!
This is fun!

Ça c'est super!
Ça c'est marrant!

Oh dear! Goodbye, balloons!

Oh mon dieu! Au revoir, les ballons!

Have you lost your balloon?
Never mind, don't cry!

Tu as perdu ton ballon?
Ce n'est pas grave! Ne pleure pas!

Are you hungry?
Have some cake.

Vous avez faim? Prenez du gâteau.

Are you thirsty?
Have a drink.

Tu as soif? Sers-toi à boire.

That was a lovely party.
Thank you for having us.

C'était une chouette fête.
Merci pour l'invitation.

Look! The balloons!

Regardez! Les ballons!

Goodbye!

Au revoir!

Pronouncing French

Don't worry if your pronunciation isn't quite correct. The important thing is to be willing to try. The pronunciation guide here will help but it cannot be completely accurate:

• Read the guide as naturally as possible, as if it were British English.

• Put stress on the letters in *italics* e.g. lombool-*onss*.

• Don't roll the r at the end of the word, for example in the French word **le** (the): ler.

If you can, ask a French person to help and move on as soon as possible to speaking the words without the guide.

Words Les Mots

leh moh

happy birthday!
bon anniversaire!

boh an-ee-vair-*sair*

cake
le gâteau

ler gat-*o*

present
le cadeau

ler cad-*o*

balloon
le ballon
ler bah-*loh*

bubble
la bulle de savon
lah b'yool der sav*oh*

mask
le masque
ler mask

hi
salut
sal-*yoo*

hello
bonjour
boh-*shoor*

thank you
merci
mair*see*

dinosaur
le dinosaure
ler deeno-*zor*

goodbye
au revoir
oh r'v*wah*

friend
l'ami, l'amie
lam*ee*, lam*ee*

lovely
chouette
shoo-*et*

brilliant
génial
shen-*yal*

fantastic
super
s'yoo*pair*

fun
marrant
marr*oh*

party
la fête
lah fett

red
rouge
roo-jsh

purple
violet
vee-o-*leh*

blue
bleu
bl'

green
vert
vair

A simple guide to pronouncing this French story

C'est mon anniversaire.
seh mon an-ee-vair-*sair*

Voilà tous mes amis.
vwul-*a* too meh zam*ee*

Salut! Bonjour! Entrez tous!
sal*yoo*, boh-*shoor*, ontreh tooss

Tous ces cadeaux pour moi?
too seh cad-*o* poor mwah

Quel masque génial!
kel mask shen-*yal*

Et j'adore ce dinosaure!
eh shah-*door* ser deeno-*zor*

Si on faisait des bulles de savon?
see oh feh-*seh* deh b'yool der sav*oh*

Elles sont belles, non?
el soh bel, noh

un, deux, trois, quatre, cinq, six, sept, huit, neuf, dix
ahn, der, trwah, catr', sank, seess, set, weet, nerf, deess

Oh là là!
o, lah, lah

Où sont-elles passées?
oo son tel pass-*eh*

Eh! Regardez Sarah!
eh, rer-gard-*eh* sah-*rah*

Des ballons!
deh bah-*loh*

Est-ce que je peux en avoir un?
essker sh' per on avwah ahn

Le rouge est pour toi.
ler roo-jsh eh poor twah

Le vert est pour moi.
ler vair eh poor mwah

Le bleu est pour Pierre.
ler bl' eh poor pee-*air*

Le violet est pour Claire.
ler vee-o-*leh* eh poor claire

Ça c'est super!
sah seh s'yoo*pair*

Ça c'est marrant!
seh marr*oh*

Oh mon dieu!
oh moh d'yer

Au revoir, les ballons!
oh r'v*wah* leh bah-*loh*

Tu as perdu ton ballon?
too ah pair*doo* toh bah-*loh*

Ce n'est pas grave! Ne pleure pas!
ser neh pah grahv, ner pler pah

Vous avez faim?
vooz av*eh* fah

Prenez du gâteau.
pr'n*eh* dew gat-*o*

Tu as soif?
too ah swuf

Sers-toi à boire.
sair twah ah bwah

C'était une chouette fête.
seh-*tet* yoon shoo-*et* fet

Merci pour l'invitation
*mair*see poor lanveet-assee-*oh*

Regardez! Les ballons!
rer-gard-*eh*, leh bah-*loh*

Au revoir!
oh r'v*wah*